Puppet Shows

by the same author

PRACTICAL LESSONS IN MAGIC
MAKING A SHADOWGRAPH SHOW
THE ART OF PAPER TEARING
CONJURING

Puppet Shows to Make

How to entertain with all kinds of puppets

ERIC HAWKESWORTH

Illustrated by
Margaret and Eric Hawkesworth

FABER AND FABER
3 Queen Square
London

*First published in 1972
by Faber and Faber Limited
3 Queen Square London WC1
Printed in Great Britain by
Latimer Trend & Co Ltd Plymouth
All rights reserved*

ISBN 0 571 09836 3

© *Eric Hawkesworth 1972*

*This book is dedicated to
Geoffrey, Vera, Michael
and Doris*

Contents

Foreword	*page* 9
A Punch and Judy Show	11
Making a portable booth and the glove puppets	
Mr Punch and the Haunted Valley	
Living Marionettes	31
Mr Song and Dance Man	
Clown in a Circus	
A Finger Puppet Theatre	44
Making the theatre and finger puppets	
Wild West story	
TV Shadow Puppets	55
A TV shadow screen and cardboard puppets	
The London to Paris Race	
A Rod Puppet Show	66
How to make simple puppets	
The School Concert	
The Skeleton in the Cupboard	76
A portable stage and string marionettes	
The Treasure of Captain Kidd	

Contents

An Evening with Puppets *page* 91
How to present a puppet variety show

Foreword

These practical instructions are written to teach the amateur performer the whole art of entertaining with puppets, and will enable him to construct, direct and stage-manage the miniature actors through complete routines.

Simple but effective methods of building make for inexpensive home construction and a new range of portable booths, puppet stages and model theatres present the shows with professional effect. The book contains working examples of almost every type of marionette.

Each section of the book describes a complete act using a particular form of puppet—glove, 'living' marionette, finger, shadow, rod and string—and a patter and performing script is included so that the words and actions can be practised together. In no other field of entertainment is it more important to match proficient manipulation with music, dialogue and sound effects to create effectively the illusion of real-life characters.

All the routines are original with up-to-date story plots to suit contemporary audiences and even Mr. Punch is written with the traditional scenes and characters scripted to the modern idiom. Programme notes, with practical suggestions for staging, lighting and pre-recording the sound effects, etc., are given for presenting a complete 'night of puppets' entertainment.

A Punch and Judy Show

Glove puppets play a major role in the world of entertainment and their methods of presentation are many and varied to suit modern requirements. Today's performers tend to dispense with heavy and elaborate puppet theatres and manipulate the figures in full view of the audience using various masking devices to help preserve the illusion. Sometimes the glove puppet is worked inside a top hat—a hole is cut in the side for insertion of the hand—and often the performer is concealed under a table with the glove protruding through a cut-away portion of the table top. *Punch and Judy*—the classic glove-puppet show—still needs a booth for best effect and the one described incorporates several novel features. The lightweight all-folding frame can be assembled in a few minutes and the performing shelf is brought down to a low level to give the audience a better view of the show. The operator works from a comfortable seated position with his face concealed behind a lace backcloth. This way he has good control of the puppets and it is possible to produce the voice sounds from the right place at the back of the figures. The puppets hang in a rack immediately in front of the performer and a kazoo squeaker is fixed by a wire to the frame and conveniently placed near the operator's lips for the production of Mr. Punch's characteristic voice. The old-style Punch booth—more than seven feet high—was quite impractical for shows in the average home but this low-level booth opens up a considerable field of private home engagements.

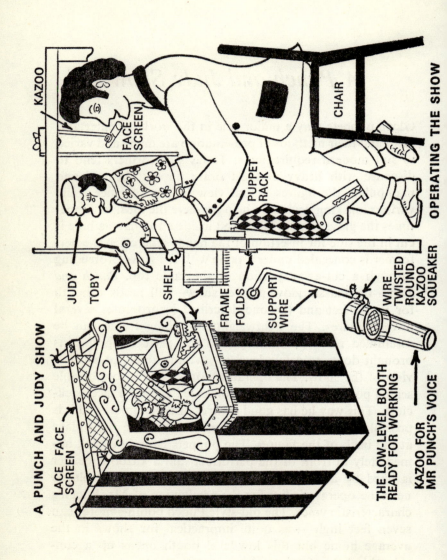

A Punch and Judy Show

Making the Frame

Planed timber of 2-inch (50-mm.) by 1-inch (25-mm.) section is used to make the six folding frames and the drawing shows how these are all assembled using simple sawn halving joints glued and screwed together. The two centre frames—upper and lower—each measure 2 feet wide (600 mm.) by 2 feet 3 inches (675 mm.) high and the four side frames all measure 22 inches (550 mm.) wide by 2 feet 3 inches (675 mm.) high. An extra thickening strip of the same section wood is screwed to the rear of one side of each centre frame as shown to permit the frames to fold flat after hingeing. Ten butt hinges measuring 2 inches (50 mm.) by $\frac{3}{4}$ inch (18 mm.) are used to assemble the six frames and these are screwed in the positions indicated—hanging a pair of side frames to each of the centre frames. Because of the extra thickening strips provided, the side frames can be folded quite flat in the sequence shown. The upper unit of three frames is then hinged to the lower set with a pair of face-mounted hinges. Coachbolts with washers and wingnuts—these are $\frac{1}{4}$-inch (6-mm.) diameter bolts put through drilled clearance holes in the frames—lock the unit in the opened position and a top stay bar is bolted across the frame tops to act as a brace and also support the face screen. This stay bar is 2 feet 9 inches (825 mm.) long and is set 12 inches (300 mm.) back from the centre frame.

A cover for the frame is made from striped canvas material to the dimensions given—4 feet 6 inches (1,350 mm.) deep by 6 feet (1,800 mm.) wide and the performing opening is 16 inches (400 mm.) deep by 24 inches (600 mm.) wide. The stripes should run vertically for best effect and any raw edges of the material turned up and hemmed. Eight pieces of tape—each 18 inches (450 mm.) long—are doubled and

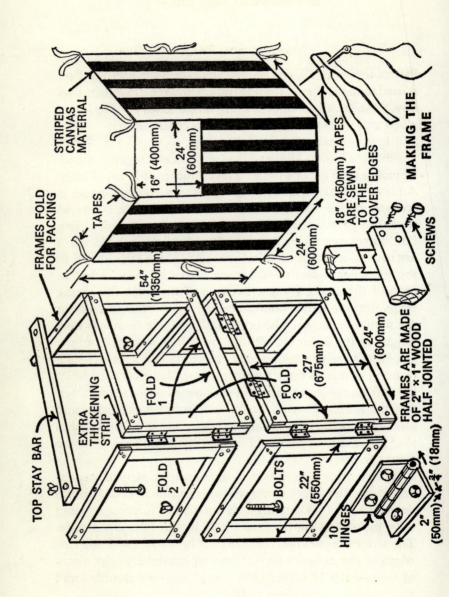

A Punch and Judy Show

strongly stitched to the points indicated. When the cover is finished it can be added to the frame.

This completes the basic booth and cover assembly, and the canvas is now removed so that the folding frames can be primed and painted, using a wood undercoat followed by two coats of matt black paint.

FACEBOARD AND PUPPET RACK

The faceboard is cut from a sheet of thin ply—not less than $\frac{3}{16}$-inch (4-mm.) thickness—and measures, before marking out, 30 inches (750 mm.) wide by 22 inches (550 mm.) high. First, pencil in the stage opening as a rectangle 14 inches (350 mm.) high by 20 inches (500 mm.) wide, setting this 2 inches (50 mm.) up from the bottom of the sheet. Then draw in the side curtains as shown. Copy the curved outline of the faceboard, then fret-saw to shape and sand paper all the sawn edges. Make the performing shelf from $\frac{1}{2}$-inch (12·5-mm.) thick plywood, rounding off the front corners and notching to fit into the stage opening, then bolt it to a 2-inch (50-mm.) square wood strip 15 inches (375 mm.) long which is screwed to the faceboard. Prime the bare wood with a suitable undercoat and paint the faceboard and shelf red. Use an artist's brush to paint in the decorative scrolls in gold paint making them about $\frac{1}{4}$-inch (6-mm.) thick. Affix a fringed blue velvet drape to the front of the performing shelf using brass dome-headed furniture tacks and paint the stage side curtains blue to match the shelf drape. Two coach-bolts with wingnuts secure the completed faceboard to the frame. Correctly positioned, the top edge of the faceboard opening should be level with the under side edge of the centre frame.

Make the puppet rack from a strip of $\frac{1}{2}$-inch (12·5-mm.) plywood 20 inches (500 mm.) long by 3 inches (75 mm.)

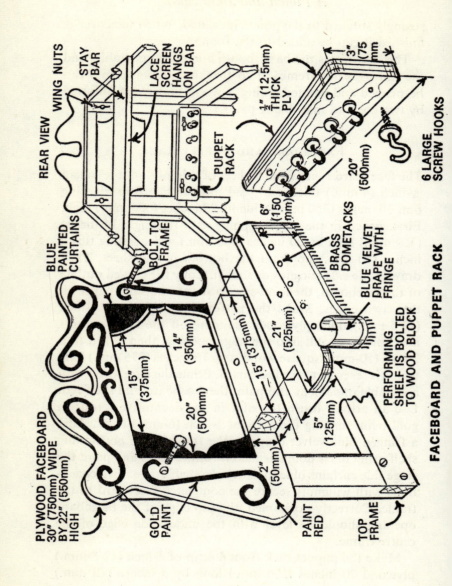

FACEBOARD AND PUPPET RACK

A Punch and Judy Show

deep and space out six large screw cup-hooks along its centre line. Bolt the rack to the lower bar of the top centre frame. Then complete the booth by hanging the lace backcloth to the stay bar. Any close-mesh window curtain lace is suitable and may be dyed dark green to give a good backing effect to the show.

Instead of the conventional punch-call reed for the production of Mr. Punch's squeaky voice, a musical kazoo is wired to the stay bar as shown, conveniently placed for the operator to talk through. This makes an excellent substitute for the mouth reed and, with very little practice, enables Mr. Punch's squeaks and squawks to be reproduced quite realistically.

MAKING THE PUPPETS

Because of the need for robust handling in the various scenes, Punch and Judy puppet heads are traditionally hand carved from solid wood, but this is not an easy method for the home constructor. All the heads in the following set are built up from thin plywood using a method that provides a good finger mounting plus a solid, three-dimensional appearance. Care in finishing and painting the heads and dressing the puppets will provide the performer with a smart and serviceable set of figures. Five puppets and a range of accessories are described—the minimum needed for a show —but other puppets may be added later using the same general methods of construction.

Mr. Punch

Mark out Mr. Punch's head on a 3-inch (75-mm.) square of $\frac{1}{8}$-inch (3-mm.) thick plywood using the grid of $\frac{1}{2}$-inch (12·5-mm.) squares shown on the drawing as a guide. Notice how the head shape has small grooves provided at neck and

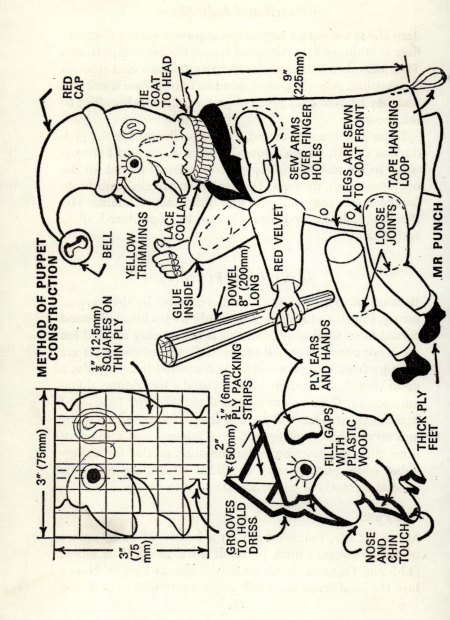

A Punch and Judy Show

hat line to provide fixing points for glove bodies and head gear. Neatly saw out the shape, then use the piece to draw a second profile. The two completed ply heads are assembled as shown using a 2-inch (50-mm.) wide back spacer as a packing strip after carefully feathering the noses and chins to fit flush. Use a suitable wood glue plus a few small panel pins to hold the pieces firmly. Insert another packing strip of plywood to form the finger-hole then build up the face with plastic filler material—plastic wood is ideal for modelling the details. Add plywood ears then prime and paint the head using reddish pink as a base and putting in hair, mouth and eyes with black, red and blue paint. Cheeks and ears can be coloured up with a little red paint on a finger.

Mr. Punch's coat is a tapering tube of red velvet 9 inches (225 mm.) long and is fixed to the wooden head by a draw thread pulled round the neck grooves. The glove is tried on the operator's hand at this stage and the positions marked for the thumb and second finger holes. Short tubes of red velvet are sewn over these holes to form the puppet's arms and plywood hands are glued into the cuffs as shown. A lace ruff collar is folded up from a strip of tape and is stitched over the drawstring, then lapel facings and buttons are added. Mr. Punch is the only puppet with legs and these are padded tubes of red velvet, very loosely jointed at the knees. They are fitted with plywood shoes and the legs are then sewn to the front of the glove—again with very loose joints. Pieces of coat material are sewn to make the cap which is padded and trimmed with yellow ribbon and bell. A stick of ½-inch (12·5 mm.) dowel 8 inches (200 mm.) long is needed for Mr. Punch to carry. A loop of strong tape is attached to the base of the glove for hanging up the puppet when not in use.

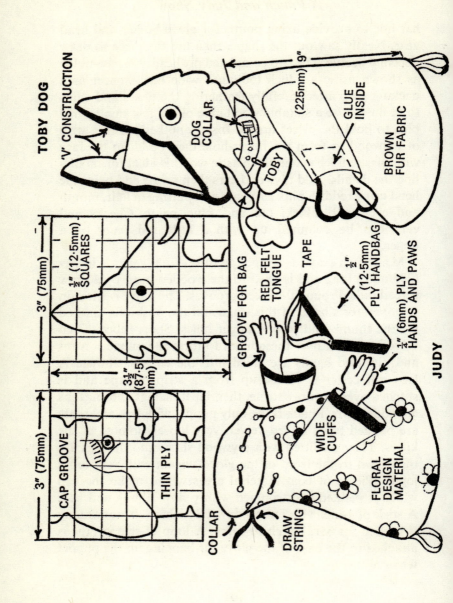

A Punch and Judy Show

Judy

Judy's head is constructed exactly like Mr. Punch's again marking out on 3-inch (75-mm.) plywood squares. Her dress is made of a bold floral design material—same dimensions as before—and it has a stand-up collar with a drawstring and wide flared sleeves. Judy's hands are set into the cuffs and glued and the left wrist is grooved to carry a handbag made of ½-inch (12·5 mm.) ply. This handbag with its tape handle is not fixed permanently to Judy's hand so that it can be removed for certain scenes. Make her mob cap from a disc of the dress material—4 inches (100 mm.) in diameter—turned over a cloth pad and sewn in position.

Toby Dog

Plywood pieces measuring 3 inches (75 mm.) by 3½ inches (87·5 mm.) are used to shape this puppet's head and the only variation from the other figures is the insertion of a plywood V piece into the top of the head as shown. Paint the head light brown with white markings and, after adding the brown fur-fabric glove body, fit a dog collar round the neck. Glue a red felt 'tongue' into the jaw and add a large ply name disc to the collar. Plywood paws—painted white—and a tape hanging loop complete the puppet.

Policeman

Dark blue material is used to make the glove body for this figure which is attached in the usual way by a draw-string to the wooden head. The letters and numbers PC 99 are embroidered in white cotton on a strip of the blue cloth and the collar is sewn round the neck of the policeman. The truncheon and handcuffs are cut out with the hands in one piece although the bottom part of the wrist cuffs are attached via a short piece of watch chain. Silver buttons are

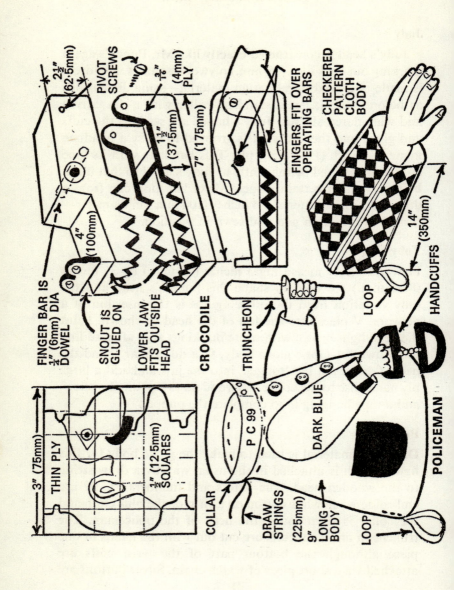

A Punch and Judy Show

sewn down the front of the coat. Make the helmet from dark blue felt—cutting two bell-shaped sections and sewing together. See illustration of Punch Show Accessories. Pad the helmet and fix a silver star to its front before glueing to the head of the puppet.

Crocodile

The crocodile's head and jaw is built up from $\frac{5}{16}$-inch (4-mm.) thick plywood with the lower jaw fitting outside the upper part of the head. Make each part as shown, then pivot them together using a pair of short woodscrews. Two bars are fitted into the head—one is a length of $\frac{1}{4}$-inch (6-mm.) dowel and the other a strip of ply—so that the fingers and thumb can operate the jaw in a snapping action. Make the crocodile's body from a tube of checkered pattern cloth 14 inches (350 mm.) long and glue and tack it to the wooden head. Make all the glove tubes very full at the outer end for ease of operation. Finish the crocodile by glueing a plywood snout to the upper jaw and painting the head black with white eyes and teeth.

PUNCH SHOW ACCESSORIES

The baby carriage is a shaped plywood box 4 inches (100 mm.) long by $2\frac{1}{2}$ inches (62·5 mm.) wide and it has four plywood discs glued to the sides as shown. The handle is fixed to a pair of curved arms which are screwed to the carriage sides. Paint the body blue and the wheels white with black spokes.

Baby is a 3-inch (75 mm.) tube of blue velvet—$1\frac{1}{2}$ inches (37·5 mm.) in diameter at the bottom end tapering to a snug fit on to the flat plywood head. A strip of blue velvet forms a bonnet and the arms are simple rolls of the same material sewn in place. Three small buttons are sewn down the front of the gown.

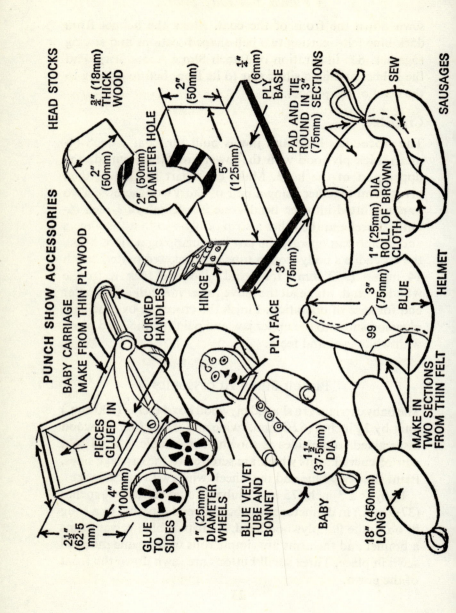

A Punch and Judy Show

The head stocks replace the out-dated gallows scene but still retain the same comic effect. Make the stocks from ¾-inch (18-mm.) thick wood—each half is 5 inches (125 mm.) long by 2 inches (50 mm.) deep and has a semi-circular hole cut in the middle as shown, to form a 2-inch (50-mm.) diameter head hole when the sections are together. Screw a hinge at one side and fix the stocks to a base plate of thin plywood measuring 5 inches (125 mm.) by 3 inches (75 mm.).

The string of sausages is made from an 18-inch (450-mm.) strip of brown cloth sewn into an inch (25 mm.) diameter tube. The tube is then padded in 3-inch (75 mm.) sections and tied between sections. Fit a tape loop for hanging up the sausage string.

Preparing the Show

The operator sits behind the booth with his face level with the stage opening but concealed by the face screen. The puppets are hung across the rack from left to right in the following order: Crocodile, Judy, Policeman, Toby, Sausages and Baby—on the same hook—and finally, Mr. Punch. The accessories are laid out: Mr. Punch's stick, Judy's handbag and the pram are on the performer's lap and head stocks are down on the floor to the performer's left hand side. The chairs for the audience should be set out to leave a clear six-foot gap between the front row and the booth. A large white handkerchief should be placed in the operator's breast pocket.

Performing the Show: What to Say and Do

Mr. Punch and the Haunted Valley

The show is introduced by the Policeman puppet which is

A Punch and Judy Show

lifted into view on the performer's left hand. He looks at the audience and bows, then speaks in a gruff voice:

'Evening all! I'm Police Constable 99 . . . and this is my patrol. With my handcuffs and my truncheon . . . I must uphold the law!'

Make the puppet walk, in a series of up and down bobs, from left to right across the performing shelf and back again. The handcuffs and truncheon are shaken to illustrate the patter then the Policeman turns and waves his truncheon towards the back of the stage:

'Mr. Punch and his wife Judy live in the house over there . . . it's a wonder you can't hear them shouting! I'm always telling them to be quiet . . . but today, they are going on a picnic, into the country. I'm going to follow them to make sure they keep the peace . . . but first, let us look into their house where we shall see Judy getting her baby ready.'

The Policeman is lowered out of sight and the glove removed and hung on its hook. Judy is fitted on the left hand and Mr. Punch on the right, then Judy makes her appearance:

'Hello everybody! . . . What a beautiful day for a picnic . . . I've so much to do before we can go! . . . baby to get ready! . . . sandwiches to pack! . . . and idle Mr. Punch doesn't help at all! I must fetch the pram and put the baby to sleep!'

Judy takes the pram from the performer's lap and places it on the shelf. Next, she fetches the baby puppet off its hook and places it in the pram. She sings 'Rock-a-Bye Baby' as she tips the pram back and forth but soon grows impatient and starts calling for Mr. Punch to come and help:

'Mr. Punch! Mr. Punch! . . . Where is that idle-bones Mr. Punch! Come and help me put the baby to sleep! . . . We shall never be ready!'

Mr. Punch appears with his stick and occupies the right-

A Punch and Judy Show

hand side of the stage. His voice is heard off-stage before the puppet is shown saying:

'La-de-da-de-da! What's to do! What's to do! Hello everybody!'

Mr. Punch beats the stage with his stick then drops it on to the performer's lap. Judy tells him he must get the baby to sleep while she prepares the sandwiches, then she disappears below. Mr. Punch squeaks and squawks and sings, 'Go to sleep my baby' as he rocks the pram violently but soon he takes the baby out of the pram and lays it down at the left-hand side of the shelf. The pram is knocked back on to the performer's lap and can be disposed on to the floor. The Judy glove is pulled off the left hand and the first two fingers of this hand are placed inside the gown of the baby as Mr. Punch picks up the doll to make it 'walk'. This puppet is made to move from left to right across the back of the shelf and each time, Mr. Punch pushes the baby back to its corner to try again:

'Come on baby! . . . Walkey walkey walkey! . . . We're going on a picnic so walkey walkey walkey!'

Mr. Punch knocks the baby back on to the performer's lap, he himself disappears below the shelf. The Judy glove is fitted on to the right hand—with the handbag over the wrist—and Toby Dog on the left hand. Always replace the puppets on the hooks as soon as both hands are free during a double change. Place the sausage string on the lap ready for working, then bring Judy into view:

'At last . . . the sandwiches are packed in my bag and we are ready to set off into the country. Mr. Punch has gone ahead . . . but where is our dog Toby? Toby! Toby! . . . Come on Toby!'

Raise the Toby puppet as Judy explains that Toby can talk by wuffing once for 'Yes' and twice for 'No'. She asks Toby if he wishes to go on the picnic to which he replies

A Punch and Judy Show

'Wuff!' Judy says it will be a long walk ... what will he take to eat? Toby vanishes inside the booth ... and returns holding the string of sausages. Judy says she will see everybody at the picnic and then both puppets are lowered.

Country Scene

After a brief pause, the Policeman puppet is raised on the right hand and he sets the scene for the second act:

'Hello again! Here we are ... out in the country ... and Mr. Punch and Judy together with their dog Toby will be along any minute. I don't want to scare Mr. Punch ... but he has chosen this haunted valley for his picnic spot! Behind me is a dark, mysterious cave ... with a ghost! ... and over there is a lake ... with a phantom crocodile! It gives me the shivers just to think about it! I'm going to hide behind this tree and see what happens! Please don't tell Mr. Punch about the ghosts ... he really isn't very brave!'

Withdraw the Policeman figure and change it to Mr. Punch. Fit the Toby Dog puppet on to the left hand and drape a white handkerchief over the dog's head. Raise Mr. Punch into the stage opening and let him say:

'Ghosts! Ghosts! Did someone say ... Ghosts! I can't see any ghosts!'

Bring the covered Toby up behind Mr. Punch and let him follow wherever Mr. Punch moves. The audience will quickly shout and tell Mr. Punch about the ghost ... but whenever he turns round, the white cloaked figure vanishes below stage. The move is repeated several times till finally Mr. Punch pulls off the cover to reveal Toby. Mr. Punch fetches his stick and chases Toby all round the stage until he eventually knocks the dog down into the booth, shouting:

'That's the way to do it! ... That's the way to do it!'

Toby is changed to Judy who comes up yelling:

A Punch and Judy Show

'Shame on you, Mr. Punch! . . . Pick on someone your own size!'

Judy swings her handbag at Mr. Punch and they fight all over the stage. Judy is dropped on to the performer's lap as Mr. Punch calls:

'That's the way to do it! . . . That's the way to do it!'

The Policeman now enters the play—on the left hand—in place of Judy and he speaks sternly to Mr. Punch:

'You villain, Mr. Punch! . . . I saw what you did to Judy and Toby! . . . I was hiding right behind that tree! I must take you into custody!'

Mr. Punch waves his stick in anger and shouts:

'Custard! Custard! . . . I don't want to go in any custard!'

The Policeman goes below and returns with the head stocks which he places centre stage. He opens the top stock and tells Mr. Punch to put his head in the hole. Mr. Punch acts stupid and places his head first to one side of the stocks . . . then the other. The policeman shakes his truncheon and cries:

'NO! NO! NO! . . . Silly Mr. Punch! Put your head through the hole! . . . Not by the side of it! Here! . . . Let me show you!'

When the Policeman places his neck in the stocks, Mr. Punch promptly slams them together and shouts:

'That's the way to do it! . . . That's the way to do it!'

The Policeman and stocks are cleared away into the booth and the left hand slides into the Crocodile puppet. Mr. Punch struts about the stage and then sits with his legs across the shelf in the right-hand corner. Slowly, the Crocodile is raised and the head is laid on the performing shelf. Mr. Punch comes across and strokes the Crocodile with his stick saying:

'Why! . . . It's a nice pussy cat! Come here, nice pussy cat!'

A Punch and Judy Show

The audience will quickly enlighten Mr. Punch as they call out to tell him what it really is! Indeed, they should be encouraged to participate right through the show. Usually, their sympathies will be against Mr. Punch and there are many opportunities to direct their calls in this fashion.

The Crocodile seizes Mr. Punch's stick in its teeth and throws it into the booth. Then Mr. Punch fetches the string of sausages and offers it to the Crocodile. Again the creature grips the string and throws it into the booth. Then Mr. Punch and the Crocodile grapple and fight for a few seconds. They vanish down into the booth but are back in a moment . . . this time Mr. Punch is sitting astride the Crocodile's back for an amusing finish!

The Judy glove replaces the crocodile puppet and Mr. Punch and Judy take their bow by saying alternate lines, with Judy speaking first:

> 'Our play is over and we have to go,
> We hope that you enjoyed the show!
> The quarrels and fights were only pretend,
> So kiss me Judy . . . and let's be friends!'

ADDITIONAL PUNCH AND JUDY CHARACTERS

A great variety of other characters are added to Punch and Judy shows to fill out the basic plot which is several hundred years old and many of the original dozen or so characters have changed their image to suit modern audiences. A clown, ghost, skeleton, prison warder and a town crier can be used in various scenes and a popular interlude comprises two boxers who come on midway through the show to do battle for a few rounds. Usually one is named after a world champion and the other after a well-known local boxing hero and the stage is set by using a pair of short posts that slot into square holes in the performing shelf with a piece of white rope tied across to represent the boxing ring.

Living Marionettes

The performer's head is mated to a miniature puppet body to form this highly effective, but rather neglected, type of marionette show. When properly staged and presented, the effect is extremely deceptive and indeed, living marionettes were displayed in sideshows of English fairgrounds for many years under the billing 'The Smallest Man in the World'. Two examples are detailed—one is for easy home construction and presentation in which the miniature figure does a song and dance routine using a table and draped doorway as a simple setting, but the second show is presented in a portable, fold-up theatre complete with tableau curtains and travelling backcloth to give the full range of effects. Here a clown puppet performs a series of tricks including walking on a ball, swinging on a trapeze and riding a unicycle.

A Living Marionette

Make the body from a 12-inch (300-mm.) square of thin plywood and fretsaw it to shape after marking the outline as shown in the sketch. Notice how the collar is cut to a curve to fit round the performer's neck and how the jacket flares out from the shoulders to the full 12-inch (300-mm.) width across the base of the coat. The details of collar, coat and tie can be painted in after priming the new wood with a suitable undercoat and real buttons can be fixed with contact adhesive. Make the jacket yellow with red

Living Marionettes

braided outline and paint the tie in brightly contrasting colours. The collar is finished white. Arms for the marionette are tubes of yellow material, shaped and padded as shown, then sewn to the plywood body after drilling a series of small holes at shoulder level to pass the needle and thread through. Padded white cotton gloves with the fingers sewn down naturally are added to the arms and the right glove holds a cane made from a 12-inch (300-mm.) length of ⅜-inch (9-mm.) diameter wood dowel. The knob for the cane is a disc of plywood tacked and glued to the upper end, and then the stick is painted silver with a black ferrule. Glue and stitch the cane into the glove at a point 4 inches (100 mm.) down from the knob. Striped canvas strips 12 inches (300 mm.) long by 8 inches (200 mm.) wide—deck-chair material is ideal—are used to make the legs and these are turned in 1 inch (25 mm.) at each side for a short distance near the tops before glueing to the back of the plywood jacket. The sketch shows how the puppet's feet are activated by the performer's hands through the backcloth so the feet are made in the form of boxes to accommodate each hand. Make the feet boxes from thin plywood assembled with glue and panel pins to be an easy fit on the hand. Dimensions given are suitable for the average adult hand but these may be altered to give a better fit where necessary. Paint the boxes black then glue them to the bottoms of the canvas legs after snipping out a section of the material as shown. This cut-out section fits across the box and the canvas sides are turned back and glued to give a three-dimensional appearance to the legs. Attach a pair of tie cords to the collar of the marionette for fixing to the performer's neck and obtain a straw hat of correct size to complete the figure and accessories.

C

Living Marionettes

SETTING UP THE SHOW

Drape a pair of full-length curtains over an open doorway and pin them together leaving gaps for head and hands. Choose a table for the stage and place this immediately in front of the curtains as shown. It may be necessary to adjust the height of the performer in relation to the stage so that he can work comfortably. Either the stage height can be adjusted or the performer can stand on a box or low stool to obtain the right level. If the show is being set up in view of an audience then a screen is needed while the performer gets the marionette in position through the curtain gaps. When all is ready and the figure is firmly attached to the performer's neck with straw hat at a jaunty tilt and hands tucked into the feet boxes, an assistant can remove the screen ready for the show.

PERFORMING THE SHOW: WHAT TO SAY AND DO

'Hello everybody . . . I'm Tiny Tom Thumb!
But my dancing feet are as fast as they come,
I can stand on one leg . . . and jump up in the air!
And do a tap dance . . . Just like Fred Astaire!'

Each leg is lifted in turn then the marionette apparently jumps into the air and claps its feet together before bouncing back on to the stage. Then, each foot taps out a smart rap-a-tap-tap to match the Fred Astaire line.

'But life on the stage isn't all sugar and spice,
I once had to dance Swan Lake . . . on ice!
And not many folk can stand on one toe!
Or shuffle off to Buffalo!'

The ice skating movement is simulated by gliding first one foot and then the other sideways and forward in a skating

Living Marionettes

action across the stage with the head and body following the glide. Make the marionette walk on the tips of the shoes before doing a cross-legged dance with one foot being passed, first in front and then behind the other.

> 'A song and dance man needs a very long list,
> To dance Charleston, the Polka . . . and even the Twist!
> And when he feels weary he just takes a seat,
> And looks out at the world . . . from between his feet!'

First one leg is raised and then the other to imitate the Charleston dance and the Polka is much the same except for a hopping movement. Pivot the feet on the balls of the hands to simulate the Twist. The performer then stoops to bring his head down almost to the level of the stage and holds the feet in front of his face—close together and with the soles facing towards the audience. As the end line is delivered, the feet are moved apart allowing the performer to peep between.

> 'Then it's on with the motley and on with the dance!
> The whole world is waiting . . . this may be your chance!
> The curtain goes up on act one, first scene,
> So now I'll deliver my finest routine!'

Conclude the act by singing and dancing to a popular song—your assistant can cut in some music on record or tape to provide a tuneful finish.

MAKING A PORTABLE THEATRE

The frame for the fold-up, portable theatre is constructed of planed 2-inch (50-mm.) by 1-inch (25-mm.) section timber and the corners of the three sections are assembled with half-joints as shown. Each frame is 42 inches (1,050 mm.) high with the centre unit measuring 4 feet (1,200 mm.) across and the side wings 2 feet (600 mm.). Glue and screw the corner joints for a strong construction. Then attach the side

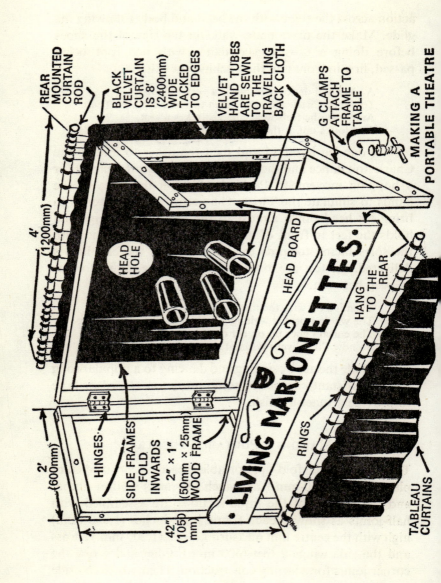

Living Marionettes

frames to the main centre frame using two pairs of butt hinges in the positions indicated. Make the headboard from a piece of ⅜-inch (9-mm.) thick plywood 4 feet (1,200 mm.) long by 6 inches (150 mm.) deep and saw it to shape after marking the outline in pencil. This headboard is bolted across the tops of the side frames using a pair of ¼-inch (6-mm.) diameter coachbolts with washers and wingnuts inside the frames. A rod for the tableau curtains is mounted at the back of the headboard using either screw eyes or a pair of drilled wood blocks and a similar rod is attached across the rear of the centre frame to carry the travelling backcloth. Two ⅜-inch (9-mm.) diameter holes are drilled in the tops of the wing frames to take the trapeze rope then the whole frame can be painted. Prime all the new wood with undercoating then paint the folding frames matt black. The headboard is painted yellow with the letters LIVING MARIONETTES put on with red transfers. The scrolls and mask of comedy are painted blue. Tableau curtains are in a heavy blue material and are hung on the rod via loosely attached curtain rings to give a good drape. A cord and pulley arrangement can be added to open and close the curtains if the performer wishes to have control of this operation—otherwise he will need another person to open and close the show. The travelling backcloth is an 8 foot length (2,400 mm.) of 42 inches (1,050 mm.) wide black material—velvet or velveteen is ideal but dyed cotton is also suitable—and this is hung on the back curtain rail using loose-fitting rings as before. A head hole is cut out in the centre of the backcloth and three hand-tubes are made and attached also. Use velvet if possible for the tubes and make them an easy fit over your hand. Each tube is 8 inches (200 mm.) long and is sewn to the backcloth over holes cut to line up with the feet and right arm of the marionette. Finally, tack each edge of the backcloth to the ends of the centre frame to complete

Living Marionettes

the theatre. Because of the extra material in the backcloth width, the performer can walk from side to side with the marionette in working position and the backcloth will follow him. This lateral movement together with the hand-tubes gives considerable freedom to manipulate the marionette through a variety of extra tricks. A pair of 'G' clamps are used to fix the theatre to a table top as shown.

A Performing Clown Marionette

The body of the clown is cut in two halves from thick yellow material to the outline given in the sketch and measures 2 feet (600 mm.) from neck to ankles with an initial width of 18 inches (450 mm.) to allow for arms and legs. Stitch the two pieces together on the wrong sides then turn the costume inside out to obtain neat joins. Lightly pad the figure using 1-inch (25-mm.) thick foam plastic cut to the shape of the clown's body. The right arm is not filled with padding but is slitted at the back of the shoulder so that the performer's arm can be inserted to operate the hand. Collar and ruffs round sleeves and trousers are cut from red felt or similar thick material and are then sewn in place. Note how the collar is open at the back with buttoned tabs for attaching to the performer's neck. A clown's hat is made of the yellow cloth and is trimmed with the red pom poms and three other red discs are sewn down the front of the costume. The plywood box feet are made as before except that the toes of the sole plate are rather longer as shown. Attach the boxes to the trouser bottoms by slitting and folding the material in the manner already described. Complete the costume by trimming the hat with lengths of thick black wool—hanging from under the brim—to simulate hair.

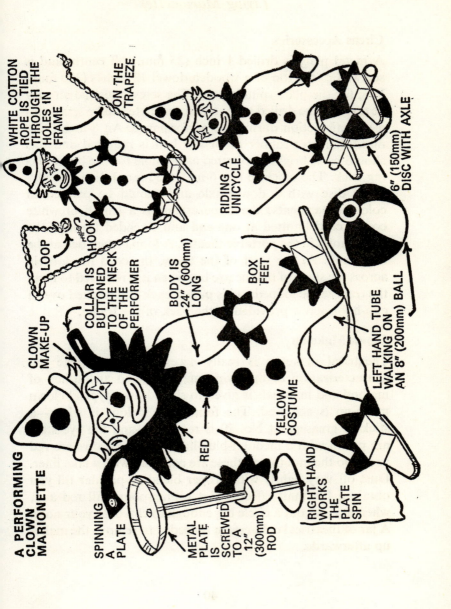

Living Marionettes

Circus Accessories

A metal plate is drilled 1 inch (25 mm.) off centre and is screwed to the top of a wooden dowel 12 inches (300 mm.) long for the plate spinning act. The screw must be an easy fit through the drilled hole so that the plate can be spun with a realistic action during the performance. An 8-inch (200-mm.) diameter rubber or plastic ball is required and this should be as brightly coloured as possible for the ball walking trick. The unicycle is a 6-inch (150-mm.) diameter plywood disc with a dowel axle and should be painted in coloured segments; the trapeze rope is a length of white cotton cord knotted at one end and threaded through the frame holes in the portable theatre. A loop is then tied at the other end. At the start of the show, the cord lies loosely across the stage of the theatre but when it is required to form the trapeze the looped end is pulled back and hooked over a cup-hook screw provided at the back of the frame.

Clown Make-up

Theatrical make-up is really necessary to complete the characterization of the living marionette so an outline of method and materials is given to show how a typical clown make-up is achieved. The foundation colour is white—a stick of greasepaint No. 20 is required—and the eye stars are put in with a medium-blue liner. The eyebrows are red as is also the mouth and these are coloured with a lake liner. Dust off very lightly with proper blending-powder till you obtain a flat matt effect. Paint a ping-pong ball red and, when dry, cut out a circle big enough to clip over your nose. A jar of theatrical cold-cream is needed to remove the make-up afterwards.

Living Marionettes

SETTING UP THE SHOW

Button the marionette round your neck after placing your head through the backcloth hole and adjust the clown hat to a firm position on your head. The trapeze cord is pulled back to lie loosely across the stage and the ball and unicycle apparatus are at the left-hand side of the stage. While the tableau curtains are still drawn, the left hand is slipped through the masking tube into the left foot and the right hand is placed into the marionette's right sleeve to grasp the plate-spinning stick through the thickness of the cloth of the puppet's hand. When the curtains are opened, the marionette is spinning the plate as shown in the performing sketch.

PERFORMING THE SHOW: WHAT TO SAY AND DO

'Howdy folks! . . . I'm Charlie the Clown, and I've come to show you some circus tricks. Do you see this plate I'm spinning? I borrowed it from our cook . . . when he wasn't looking! If I break it I'm a dead duck . . . no more dinners this week! Look out! . . . it's falling!'

The plate and stick are allowed to fall from the puppet's hand as the performer tosses them through the right-hand wing frame of the theatre to clatter on the floor of the main stage or platform. The right hand is now withdrawn from the sleeve of the marionette and pushed into the right foot box via the velvet hand tube.

'Do you like my clown boots? See how I walk on my toes and do a tap dance. I can even jump up in the air . . . and clap my feet together! One of my favourite tricks is to walk round the circus ring . . . balancing on a big ball . . . like this!'

Living Marionettes

The marionette is made to tiptoe across the stage several times with an occasional deliberate stumble and this is followed by an eccentric tap dance—crossed leg scissor actions and hopping on one leg etc.—finishing with a leap into the air and feet clapped smartly together. The performer walks the clown to the left-hand side of the stage and rolls the coloured ball back to centre stage using the left foot. Both hands are then placed on the ball so that the clown marionette can perform the balancing act. At the end of this particular section of the routine, the clown is made to kick the ball into the audience.

'Goal! . . . I scored a goal! Don't forget to give me my ball back! Oh! . . . it's great to live in a circus . . . even when the wild animals chase you! Last week a lion broke loose and ran me all round the big top! I escaped by jumping on to my one-wheel bike . . . like this!'

Walk the figure across to the unicycle and place both hands—inside the feet boxes—on to the projecting axle ends. The clown can be made to perform seemingly impossible feats of balance by leaning backwards and forwards and swivelling from side to side. Conclude the unicycle act by jumping off at speed and allowing the wheel to run to the side of the stage.

'Every circus show needs an aerial high wire act . . . watch how the trapeze rises like magic when I say the word Gazeeka—Gazooka!'

The right hand is withdrawn from the footbox for a few moments to enable the operation of the trapeze cord; the loop on the free end of this line is drawn down at the back of the theatre frame and hooked over a screw hook so that the cord hangs about 6 inches (150 mm.) off the stage. When the right hand has been replaced in the right foot box, the marionette steps on to the trapeze and swings the rope back and forth in a series of manœuvres.

Living Marionettes

'I'm the daring young man on the flying trapeze! . . . see how I balance on one leg . . . and then the other! I can even sit down on the rope as I do the splits! Let me sing as I swing, to bring our circus show to a close!'

Make the puppet stand on each leg in turn and then slide the feet outwards along the rope to do the splits. Sing one chorus of 'The Daring Young Man on the Flying Trapeze' and have the curtains pulled on the last line.

A Finger Puppet Theatre

All the thrills and excitement of a wild west rodeo are captured in this novel finger puppet theatre which has a bucking bronco, dancing bear and charging buffalo. Other characters include Big Chief Tom-Tom, the Sheriff and Mexican Pete and the plot tells how Pete plans a bank robbery while the good folk of Canyon City are watching the rodeo. The Sheriff rides fast and corners the bandit in Dead-End canyon where there is a shoot-out till Mexican Pete bites the dust. All the puppets are cut from thin cardboard and are decorated with coloured felts and the miniature theatre is complete with curtains and battery-powered footlights.

MAKING THE THEATRE

Mark out the front board on a sheet of ¼-inch (6-mm.) thick plywood measuring 15 inches (375 mm.) by 24 inches (600 mm.) noting how the top is cut in a gentle curve and the stage opening is 18 inches (450 mm.) wide by 9 inches (225 mm.) deep. Two semi-circular humps are left at the bottom of the stage opening to mask the footlight batten which is fitted to the rear of the front board as shown. Use a fret-saw to cut the plywood and smooth all the edges with fine sandpaper afterwards. The stage floor and sides are 7 inches (175 mm.) deep, front to back, and the sides are 9 inches (225 mm.) high. The whole theatre unit is assembled with a pair of wooden strips 1-inch (25-mm.) by ½-inch (12·5 mm.) section across the back of the stage—at top and bottom—so

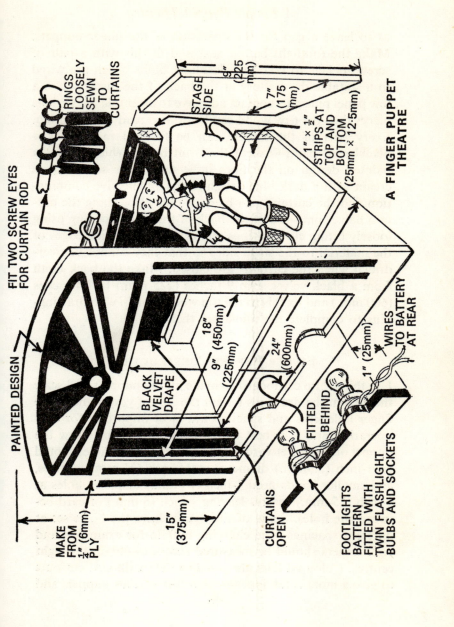

A Finger Puppet Theatre

as to leave a gap for the operation of the finger puppets. Make the footlight batten next and fit this with a pair of screw sockets to take two flashlight bulbs which are wired to a suitable dry battery at the back of the theatre. Use a few panel pins plus contact adhesive to assemble the various pieces then the new wood can be primed ready for painting. Every part of the theatre can be finished matt black—blackboard paint—except the front board which carries a painted design on the lines indicated in the sketch. Pale cream with a dark blue design forms an effective combination and the curtains can be dark blue also. Hang the curtain halves on a rod at the back of the stage opening using loosely fitting curtain rings and attach the outside edges of the material to the stage sides so that they cannot be overdrawn when the curtains are closed. Make the back cloth from a black velvet strip 9 inches (225 mm.) by 24 inches (600 mm.) and fix this to the top wooden strip with drawing-pins to complete the miniature theatre.

FINGER PUPPET CONSTRUCTION

Use thin white cardboard to make all the puppets and scale them from the drawings to suit the size of your hands. The finger hole sizes and spacings are most important for easy operation and it is best to mark these first and draw the puppet outline afterwards. For adult hands, the holes should be 1-inch (25-mm.) diameter at 1¼-inch (31-mm.) centres, and smaller hands need ¾-inch (18-mm.) diameter holes at 1-inch (25-mm.) centres leaving ¼ inch (6 mm.) of card between the holes. Some of the figures have the holes set at different spacings—the charging buffalo for example—and your fingers should be measured across to obtain the right centres. Coloured felts are glued to the cardboard cut-outs to give a more solid appearance to the various puppets and

A Finger Puppet Theatre

simple footwear is easily provided by the use of ordinary sewing thimbles.

Bucking Bronco with Rider

Mark out the two sets of finger holes on a card rectangle 7 inches (175 mm.) by 5 inches (125 mm.) and draw the bronco outline as shown. After cutting the holes and shaping the outline, the horse is cut into two pieces. The rider is cut from more card and, after decorating with felts, is fixed to the two halves by means of a pair of brass paper clips. Make the bronco a pinto by sticking black irregular-shaped patches over a white felt base. The puppet works in a most realistic action when the two hands are moved up and down in opposite movement and the horse can also be made to gallop.

Big Chief Tom-Tom

This is a standard finger puppet for operation on the first and second fingers to give a walking and dancing action. Notice how the arms are held up in the air and the feather head-dress using multicolour felts for a bright display. The Indian's coat is yellow with brown felt 'buckskin' trimmings and the facial area can be left plain card so that the details can be put in accurately with coloured inks, or using ballpoint pens. Finish the face with a red watercolour wash.

Charging Buffalo

This figure fits over the first and little fingers of the right hand as shown so the holes need spacing to suit. Use card measuring 6 inches (150 mm.) by 3 inches (75 mm.) and, after cutting out, cover it entirely with brown felt. The figure can be made to charge and toss its horns with a little practice.

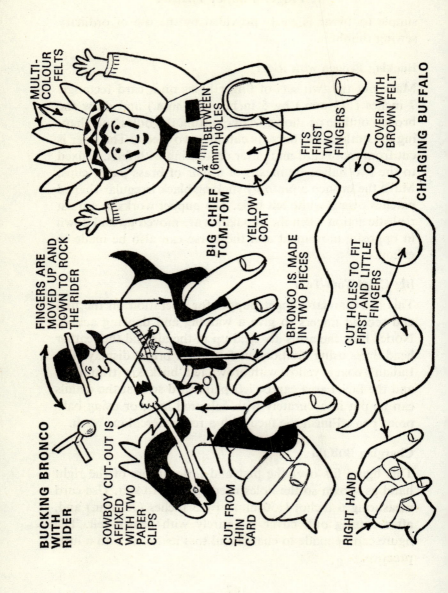

A Finger Puppet Theatre

Dancing Bear

Two sets of finger holes at the standard spacings are used for this dancing bear puppet and these accommodate the first and second fingers in the upper pair and the thumb and third finger in the lower set—little finger is curled back into the palm of the operating hand. Cover the figure with black felt and stick on the face markings with white pieces cut to shape.

Sheriff

Mark out the sheriff on a card square measuring 5 inches (125 mm.) after cutting the two finger holes. Notice how the left arm is drawn in profile and is complete with revolver; when the figure is completely finished the arm is bent forward at right angles to give a three-dimensional effect. Make the coat from brown felt and add yellow lapels, cuffs and star. Hat and collar and tie complete the trimming. The hands and face are best detailed directly on to the card and washed over with pink water-colour to give the right effect. The sheriff's boots are made from a pair of red plastic thimbles and have plywood soles glued in place after drilling holes in each wood piece to be a tight fit on the thimbles as shown. During the rodeo scene, the sheriff fights the charging buffalo in toreador style and he needs a 5-inch (125-mm.) square of red silk to drape over his gun hand.

Mexican Pete

The basic shape for this figure is very similar to the previous puppet differing only in hat shape and decoration. Also, the bandit carries his gun in his right hand so that he can 'shoot it out' with the sheriff in the final scene. The costume is mainly black with a red poncho and Pete's moustache is a shaped piece of black felt too. Silver thimbles adorn his

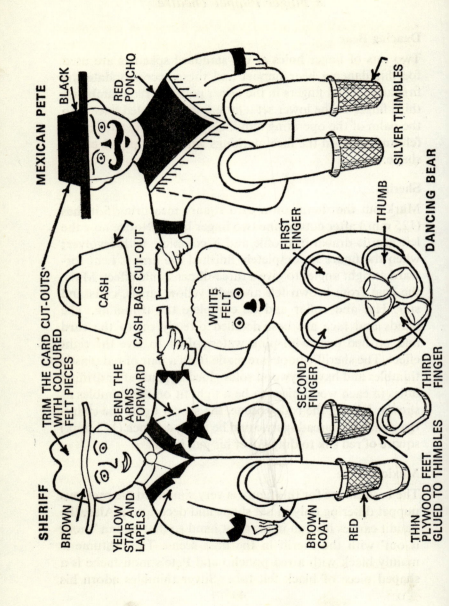

A Finger Puppet Theatre

feet and a cash bag cut-out is needed for one of the scenes. Make the handle of this bag big enough to drape over Pete's revolver which, like the sheriff's, is bent forward at the shoulder line.

Setting Up the Show

Place the miniature theatre towards the back edge of a table leaving about 4 inches (100 mm.) behind the backcloth and the table edge to serve as a ledge to hold the various puppet cut-outs and accessories. Lay out all the figures in a neat and tidy row then you are ready to connect up the footlights battery and open the front curtains.

Performing the Show: What to Say and Do

'Welcome to Canyon City in the wild and woolly west . . . the most law abiding community this side of the Rio Grande! All credit for this clean city must go to the young Sheriff who, by his daring and fearless deeds, has driven out the bandits and rustlers and made the streets and sidewalks safe for all. About the only excitement you'll find in Canyon City is the annual rodeo . . . and even here the Sheriff plays a big part. Watch him in action as he rides a Bucking Bronco . . . ride him cowboy!'

During the opening lines, the Bronco puppet is set up on the fingers of both hands and is then introduced into the theatre by dipping it under the backcloth. Make the figure walk from side to side by drumming the finger-tips in a brisk tattoo and moving the Bronco the length of the stage and backing him up again. Operate the horse in wild rodeo style by working the hands up and down in the manner described, making the rider tilt back and forth in the saddle. Remove the Bronco from the stage after a few moments and

A Finger Puppet Theatre

set up the next scene by placing the Big Chief Tom-Tom puppet on your left hand and the Dancing Bear on to the right-hand fingers. Bring the Indian into view first as you say:

'Big Chief Tom-Tom arrives from the reservation to do a traditional war dance . . . see him tap out the frenzied beat . . . first on one leg and then the other . . . pom-pom-pom-pom . . . pom-pom-pom-pom! This was the dance that brought the warriors down from the hills . . . in warpaint!'

Rap out the beat on each finger as you make the puppet do a war dance, moving the figure all over the stage and tilting him from side to side. Introduce the Dancing Bear during a pause in the dance then let the bear join in the action.

'Big Chief Tom-Tom has brought along his tame Dancing Bear . . . watch them do the Hokey-Kokey together . . . you put your right leg in, you put your right leg out . . .!'

Sing a verse and chorus of the action dance and let the two figures go through the movements, then remove them from the theatre and bring Mexican Pete into view on the fingers of the right hand. Walk him slowly across the stage to the left, gun in hand and thimbles making a measured tap.

'Out in the deserted streets of Canyon City a stranger made his way to the bank. Mexican Pete had moved across the border and his plan was to rob the bank while the townsfolk watched the rodeo. We see him enter the bank with gun in hand . . . listen as he fires a warning shot! . . . then here he comes . . . backing out of the building . . . with the cash bag on his wrist! He mounts his horse and makes a clean getaway!'

Bring the puppet to the left side of the stage and hook the cash bag over the gun hand using the left hand. Make the sound effect of a firing revolver either with a cap pistol or

A Finger Puppet Theatre

rapping a wooden ruler on the underside of the table, then back the figure the full width of the stage and off at the right-hand side. Simulate the sound of a horse riding away by drumming with the left-hand fingers in rapid tattoo on the table behind the backcloth.

'Meanwhile, back at the rodeo, the Sheriff was performing his toreador act using a red cloth . . . and a Charging Buffalo! See how he dodges the tossing horns by the merest whisper! One false step and they'd be looking for a new sheriff! Look out! . . . El Torro charges again!'

The Sheriff puppet fits on the left hand with the red silk square affixed to the gun hand by a small rubber band. First and little fingers of the right hand operate the Charging Buffalo cut-out and the figure can be made to paw the ground before charging. Repeat the movement several times and rap the Sheriff's boots on the stage as he dances out of harm's way. Remove both figures and set up the Bucking Bronco for the chase scene as you explain:

'News reached the Sheriff that the bank had been robbed so he remounted the wild Bronco and went galloping down the trail . . . telltale dust clouds up ahead indicated the bandit wasn't too far in the lead! The Sheriff thought he had a good chance of cutting the trail by the time they reached Dead-End Canyon. He must halt the thief before he reached the border!'

Slowly move the Bronco puppet right to left across the stage as you drum your fingers rapidly to imitate the flying hooves. The ride is made to swing back and forth at the same time to capture the action of the chase. Bring the Bronco out through the backcloth at the left-hand side and fit up the Sheriff—without the red silk—on the left fingers and Mexican Pete on the right. The cash bag is removed from the bandit's arm when he makes his appearance—solo—at the right of the stage.

A Finger Puppet Theatre

'Mexican Pete reached Dead-End Canyon only seconds ahead of the Sheriff and he decided to lay an ambush. With his horse tethered behind a rock and the cash packed safely in his saddle bag, Pete crouched down and waited . . . it all seemed too easy . . . soon, he would be through the canyon and safe across the border! But the Sheriff had other plans . . . he, too, had come on foot and had climbed down the canyon wall . . . to confront Mexican Pete on equal terms!'

Bring on the Sheriff at the left and let the two figures walk slowly towards each other, snapping down the fingers to rap the thimble footwear on the stage. Mexican Pete stumbles to his knees and rolls on to his side as the Sheriff proves fastest on the trigger. The right hand then withdraws the fallen bandit through the back cloth so that the performer can pull the curtains while the Sheriff takes his bow on the final scene.

'The canyon echoed with gunshot blast . . . and Mexican Pete bit the dust! The Sheriff of Canyon City had triumphed again!'

TV Shadow Puppets

The screen for this shadow theatre is built to represent a TV set and the unit is made to fold flat for easy packing. Modern techniques of shadow puppetry are employed to present a complete play in which a balloon, train and vintage car compete in a race from London to Paris and there is plenty of lively action as the scoundrel Sir Jasper attempts foul play by dropping sandbags from his balloon on to the other competitors. Cardboard cut-outs are mainly used to produce the various shadows but some of the characters are constructed with simple hand formations plus cardboard heads and other accessories to further the story plot. Pin-sharp shadows are produced by using a film strip projector but a battery-operated hand-torch with pre-focus bulb will give satisfactory results.

Making the Screen

Construct the TV screen from plywood using a panel of ¼-inch (6-mm.) thick, flat multi-ply measuring 24 inches (600 mm.) by 16 inches (400 mm.) for the front piece. Pencil out the actual screen opening, making this 19 inches (475 mm.) wide by 14 inches (350 mm.) deep and notice how this is set slightly off-centre to accommodate the dummy knobs, speaker grill and station selector at the left-hand side of the picture. Fret-saw the opening and clean up all the edges with fine sandpaper. The folding side frames are cut from ⅜-inch (9-mm.) thick ply and are produced from a

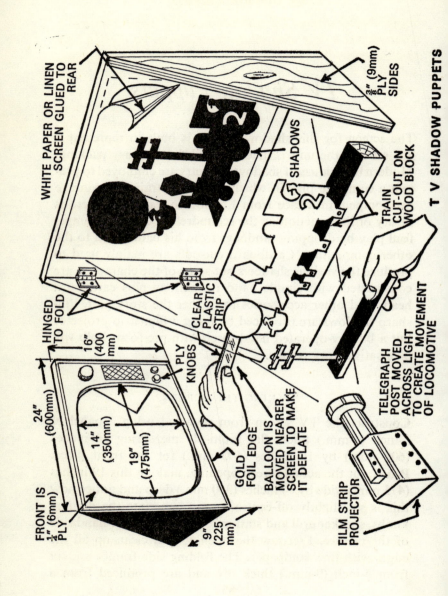

TV Shadow Puppets

single sheet 9 inches (225 mm.) wide by 16 inches (400mm.) long. Pencil a line diagonally from corner to corner and saw the panel into two pieces as shown. Clean up the edges as before then hinge the two side frames to the main panel using pairs of 1½-inch (37·5-mm.) by ½-inch (12·5-mm.) brass butts screwed inside the frame corners. Prime the new wood all over and paint all surfaces—except the front of the screen—matt black. Decorate the front of the set in realistic fashion using light brown paint as a base and treating the plywood knobs with silver metal foil. The speaker grill and frame outline are added in gold metal foil to give a smart appearance. A sheet of white paper or linen cloth is glued across the panel opening at the rear to complete the TV shadow screen. The side frames open out at right angles at the back of the screen panel to give a strong and rigid unit when the screen is set up on a table for showing.

Shadow Cut-Outs

All the shadow cut-outs are made from thin white cardboard and should be left unpainted so that the various pieces can be easily found in the semi-darkness behind the puppet screen. Mark the outlines in pencil using the drawings and dimensions as a guide then cut out the shapes cleanly with a pair of sharp scissors.

Eiffel Tower

This scene set-piece is marked on a piece of card 7 inches (175 mm.) long by 3½ inches (87·5 mm.) wide and it is important to the story plot that the top of the tower is cut to a sharp point. After shaping, the tower is tacked and glued to an inch-square wood block base to make the figure stand upright.

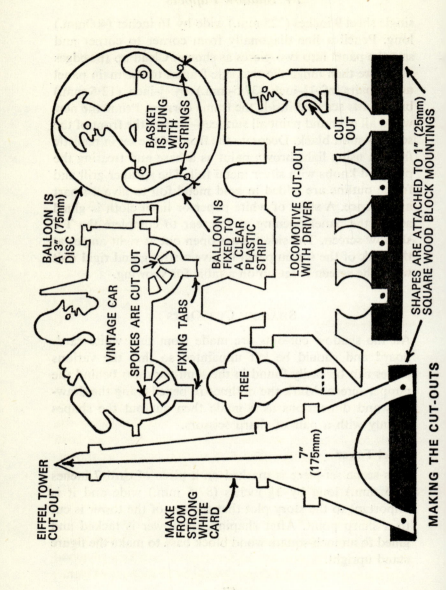

TV Shadow Puppets

Vintage Car

Use a card rectangle 5 inches (125 mm.) long by 3½ inches (87·5 mm.) deep to construct this figure and notice how the completed piece is fixed to the wooden base block by means of a pair of fixing tabs provided at the bottoms of the wheels. The spokes are cut out in the wheel centres to add a little more interesting detail.

Balloon and Basket

The balloon cut-out is a simple 3-inch (75-mm.) diameter disc and the basket, together with the outline of Sir Jasper is cut from another piece of card of about the same size. After cutting the pieces, the basket is hung from the balloon with a pair of thin strings, each 3 inches long (75 mm.). Glue the balloon disc to a strip of clear plastic 1-inch (25-mm.) wide by 12 inches (300 mm.) long so that the shadow of the figure can be projected on to the screen without visible means of support.

Locomotive

This old-time steam locomotive cut-out is complete with balloon smokestack, headlamp and cow-catcher and is made from a card piece 7 inches (175 mm.) long by 4 inches (100 mm.) deep. Fixing tabs are again provided below the wheels for mounting the shape on to a wooden block base and the number on the cabside is cut out cleanly as shown. The driver—Casey Jones—is positioned in the cab and wears a long-peaked cap.

Tree and Telegraph Post

Both the tree and telegraph post are 3 inches (75 mm.) high and, after cutting out, are each mounted on a thin plywood strip measuring 1 inch (25 mm.) wide by 12 inches (300 mm.)

TV Shadow Puppets

long. These two figures are used to create the illusion of movement to the static car and locomotive by drawing them quickly across the light beam several times.

Character Shadows and Accessories

The three main characters in the play are created with simple hand shadowgraphs plus cardboard accessories and props. The method of making and operation is shown in the sketch.

Crasher Harry

Card pieces for all the heads measure $3\frac{1}{2}$ inches (87·5 mm.) high by 3 inches (75 mm.) wide and Crasher Harry's head, with helmet, is marked and cut out leaving a thumb tab long enough to grip comfortably under the folded thumb. The vintage car driver also needs a spare wheel—make this from a 2-inch (50-mm.) diameter card disc with the spokes cut round—and a spanner which is 3 inches (75 mm.) long. Either hand can be used to make the shadow puppet, with the head shape gripped under the thumb and the first and second fingers extended to grip the various accessories.

Sir Jasper

This character is easily identified by the sun-helmet headgear and is a scaled-up version of the cut-out in the balloon basket. Sir Jasper uses a sandbag to try and stop the car and locomotive and this is a simple outline which is tied to a 12-inch (300-mm.) length of thin string, looped at the top for easy handling.

Casey Jones

Casey Jones both drives and fires the engine, and his coal shovel is cut from a card piece 4 inches (100 mm.) long by

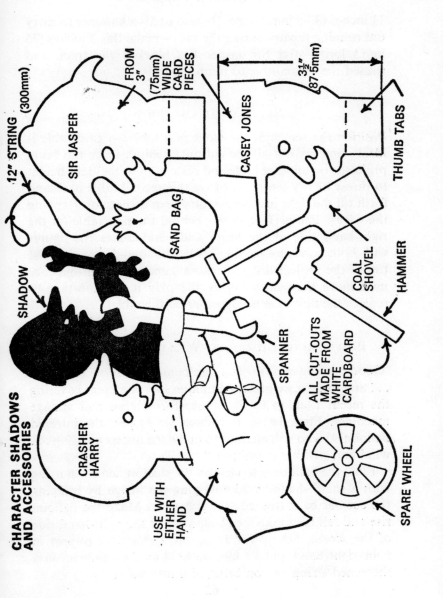

TV Shadow Puppets

1½ inches (37·5 mm.) wide. He also needs a hammer to carry out running repairs during the race—make this 3 inches (75 mm.) long—after Sir Jasper has blocked the track and caused the locomotive to jump the rails.

SETTING UP THE SHOW

Position the screen at the front of a table—a card table is ideal—and lay out all the cut-outs behind. Place the beam projector on another table and raise it up to the right height to throw its ray centrally. Move this second table back and forth till the light just covers the screen without overlapping the edges. The performer sits behind the first table on the right-hand side of the beam and manipulates the figures with both hands by passing his left hand and arm over the top of the projected ray. Because some of the cut-outs are used more than once during the play it is important to replace the figures in a tidy order on the table.

PERFORMING THE SHOW: WHAT TO SAY AND DO

'Good evening everyone! . . . welcome to shadow television . . . and tonight we present a unique sporting event covering the recent London to Paris race for veteran and vintage machines. First, let us introduce Sir Jasper, the intrepid balloonist, who will attempt to make the fastest crossing . . . wind and weather permitting!'

Float the balloon into view on the shadow screen, starting with a small shadow and enlarging the image by bringing the cut-out back towards the projector. Make the balloon rise and fall then take the shadow off at the right-hand side of the screen. Set up Sir Jasper as a character puppet in your right hand and let him be holding the sandbag on a shortened string as you bring him into view.

TV Shadow Puppets

'Here is Sir Jasper . . . complete with sun helmet and sandbag . . . and those of us who remember how this man hates to lose will know him for a dangerous competitor . . . so watch out for his underhand tricks! As Sir Jasper departs to prepare his balloon we greet another participant in the race . . . Crasher Harry, in his 1921 vintage car. Hurry up, Harry! . . . or you'll be left at the starting line!'

The car cut-out is pushed slowly across the screen then Harry is formed as a character puppet holding the spanner. This is moved up and down by bending the two fingers as you explain that Harry needs to make a few last-minute adjustments to his car before the race starts. Clear the screen then push the locomotive into view as you introduce the final character.

'From across the Atlantic comes a famous name . . . driving a vintage steam locomotive! See how Casey Jones brings his engine to a smooth halt . . . right on the starting line! Watch Casey pile on the coal with his shovel as he builds up a good head of steam for the journey!'

The locomotive is sited to the left-hand side of the screen and the character puppet is formed with the right-hand fingers holding the shovel and manipulating it at the back of the engine shadow. Remove the character puppet and take up the telegraph pole cut-out ready for the race to start.

'As the starter fired his gun, Casey opened the throttle and the locomotive picked up speed . . . see how those telegraph poles start to fly past! Soon, he was out on the main line and headed for the coast and the Channel ferry. Good luck, Casey! See you in France!'

Push the train off across the screen and replace it with the vintage car. Use the right hand to move the tree cut-out across the screen—bringing it quickly through the light ray then dipping the tree under the beam and pulling it through

TV Shadow Puppets

again. Float the balloon on to the screen above the car using the left hand as you patter:

'Out on the Dover road, Crasher Harry was making good time . . . just watch how those trees fly by! But overhead, danger lurked as Sir Jasper was overtaken. The balloonist unhitched a sandbag from the basket . . . and dropped it on to Harry's car! See how it swings down . . . then falls on to the speeding machine!'

The balloon is lifted right off the top of the screen and out of view then the sandbag is dangled in its place. The sandbag is swung over the car a few times and then allowed to fall, apparently stopping the car because the trees stop moving. Crasher Harry appears as a character puppet carrying the spare wheel which he starts to change. He fetches the spanner to tighten the new wheel . . . but he is losing valuable time.

'Harry's wheel is bent . . . and Sir Jasper flies on! Harry will have to hurry or he will miss the cross-Channel ferry! It looks as though the race will be fought between Sir Jasper and Casey Jones . . . but Casey had better watch out!'

The scene is switched to the speeding locomotive—the engine is centre screen and the telegraph poles are flying past. Again the balloon appears and a sandbag is dangled over the boiler before falling in front of the engine. Casey's locomotive is halted and he appears as a character puppet holding his hammer.

'The evil Sir Jasper repeats his trick with the sandbag .. watch how he halts Casey Jones on the main line to Paris . . . a sandbag falls on the track and the locomotive is derailed! Can nothing stop Sir Jasper winning the race! Casey Jones gets to work and straightens a wheel with his hammer . . . but he has lost so much time it is impossible to win! The engine can only limp along now!'

TV Shadow Puppets

The screen is cleared and the Eiffel Tower shadow appears on the left of the screen ready for the final scene.

'It seemed as though all Paris was waiting for the first competitor to finish . . . and the winning post was at the foot of the Eiffel Tower. Sir Jasper's balloon floated over the city . . . but in the distance could be heard the sound of Casey Jones' whistle! Watch how Sir Jasper hovers over the very point of the tower!'

The balloon silhouette is positioned over the tower cut-out with the shadows just touching. Then, the balloon shadow is made to grow smaller by moving the cut-out rapidly towards the screen . . . Sir Jasper has made an error and impaled his balloon on the very point of the tower. The locomotive cut-out is pushed on from the side and Casey Jones is the winner.

'Sir Jasper had dropped one ballast bag too many . . . and he lost control of the balloon . . . listen to the gas escape as the balloon is impaled on the tower. . . . Hiss-s-s-s! Casey Jones rolled his engine home on the last ounce of steam . . . and won the day!'

OTHER SHADOW PUPPET ROUTINES

Several other shadow puppet routines suitable for the TV shadow screen are detailed in the book *Making a Shadowgraph Show* by the same author.

A Rod Puppet Show

Three types of puppets are used to form a complete act which is presented as a novel, lecture-type entertainment. The performer shows the audience how puppets can be made from all sorts of common houshold articles and actually demonstrates their construction using a wooden spoon, a handkerchief and a folded paper square. The puppets are taken behind screen and the performer brings them to life with words and movement. The climax of the act is in the sudden appearance of the music professor which is an original type of rod puppet attached to and controlled by the performer's head. The professor conducts with baton to recorded music to bring the show to a lively finish.

Tessa the School Terror

A large wooden spoon forms the basis of this amusing puppet and a long-handled type should be chosen. The arm bar is 4 inches (100 mm.) long and is marked out on thin plywood before cutting to shape with a fret-saw. It is joined to the spoon handle 2 inches (50 mm.) below the bowl using a freely fitting bolt through drilled holes in the two pieces, and the arm bar is operated by means of a thin wire rod which is bent through another small hole drilled slightly off-centre. The bottom end of the operating rod is formed into a finger loop as shown. A school hat for the puppet is made from two pieces of dark blue felt, cut to shape and

A Rod Puppet Show

sewn round the edges at the top and sides. Lengths of thick yellow knitting wool are sewn into the hat to simulate hair, and a white felt badge completes it. The hat should be a firm fit on the wooden spoon but easy to remove. Eyes, nose and mouth are pre-cut to shape using coloured gummed paper but are not added to the spoon until the actual performance.

Making the Tunic Dress

The dress is made of dark blue felt or similar material and has white arms and sash as indicated. The skirt is pleated below the sash and the whole dress is open at the back for easy fitting over the arm bar. Two white buttons complete trimming. The puppet is operated over the top of a screen so the dress needs to be long enough to cover the performer's hand.

A Paper and Handkerchief Puppet

The head for this puppet is folded up from a paper square and the drawing shows the sequence of construction. Take an 8-inch (200-mm.) square of strong writing paper and crease it diagonally from corner to corner on both sides. Lay the sheet out flat and fold the four corners to the centre keeping all the turned in edges neatly in line. Mark the two eyes in the positions indicated with eyebrows to the centre and black them in using a ballpoint pen. Turn this packet over and again turn the corners to the middle, then the head is ready for opening. Insert the first finger and thumb into the folded corners behind the eyes and bend the packet forward as shown. This makes the standard Origami crocodile head fold and the jaw can be worked single handed by placing the first and second fingers behind the eyes and gripping the lower part of the fold between thumb and third

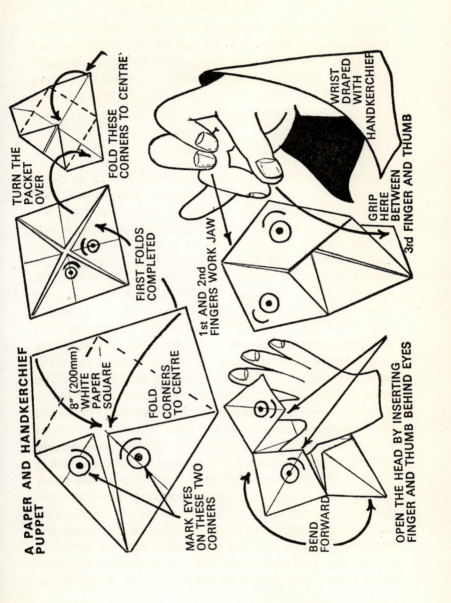

A Rod Puppet Show

finger. The hand is masked with a large pocket handkerchief—draped round the wrist and gripped under the head using the thumb and third finger which are also holding the lower jaw. The appearance and action of a paper owl is most realistic and the puppet is worked, like the previous one, over the top of a screen.

Making A Head Puppet

This puppet is tied to the performer's head leaving his hands free to wave about in true conductor fashion. Excellent control is given allowing the professor to bow and sway from side to side as he conducts the orchestra—the performer simply inclines his head in a suitable direction. Build up the puppet on a 12-inch (300-mm.) length of an inch (25 mm.) diameter wooden dowel—a broomstick handle is ideal—and use a 3-inch (75-mm.) diameter hard plastic ball for the head. Cut a hole for the dowel in one side of the ball and push the rod inside, then secure it in position with a woodscrew as shown. Two plywood discs are cut from $\frac{1}{4}$-inch (6-mm.) thick wood—one is 2 inches (50 mm.) in diameter and the other is 5 inches (125 mm.). The smaller disc is drilled to fit over the main dowel and is glued in place 7 inches (175 mm.) from the base of the rod; the large disc is screwed to the bottom to form the head platform. A thick foam plastic disc is glued to the underside of the platform and a pair of tie tapes are tacked to the top of the platform. Strands of thick brown wool are glued along each side of the head leaving a parting down the middle, and the nose is a stub of wood dowel—also fastened with contact adhesive. The eyes are painted, together with the mouth, and a pair of plastic sun glasses—without the lenses—completes the head. Make the professor's coat of any dark material—to show up the white

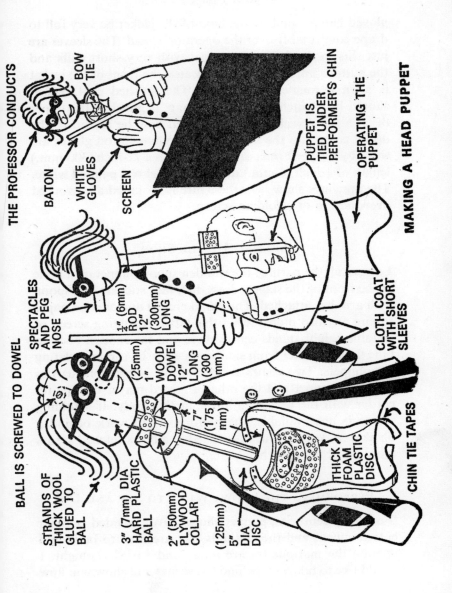

A Rod Puppet Show

gloved hands—and let the base of the jacket be very full to drape comfortably over the operator's head. The sleeves are just slits in the front of the coat with very short cuffs and the buttons are just for show because the front of the jacket is sewn permanently together. The finished coat, which should be 24 inches (600 mm.) long, is glued to the upper disc on the dowel neck. A coloured bow tie tacked to the dowel completes the head puppet. White cotton gloves are worn by the performer and the baton is a 12-inch (300-mm.) length of $\frac{1}{4}$-inch (6-mm.) diameter dowel rod painted white. The drawings show how the figure is mounted and worked over the top of a folding screen.

Setting Up the Show

Lay out all the parts of the wooden spoon puppet on a table at the front of the stage—dress, hat, face stickers and spoon with arm bar attached. The handkerchief and creased paper square are also prepared on this table. A folding screen of suitable height stands centre stage and far enough back to hide the performer from side views while he is manipulating the puppets. Two chairs are behind the screen; one carries the head puppet and the other a record player or tape recorder with the necessary music at the ready. If a folding screen is not available, the performer can work behind a blanket or curtain which is pegged to a line stretched across the stage at the right height.

Performing the Show: What to Say and Do

'For many centuries, puppet shows have provided popular entertainment and the methods that are used to build and operate the marionettes are many and varied. Tonight, I would like to take you behind the scenes and show you how

A Rod Puppet Show

simple puppets can be constructed from oddments found around the home... bits and pieces costing next to nothing!'

Hold up the wooden spoon and wiggle the arm bar with the wire control rod. Pick up the coloured paper shapes and stick them to the spoon bowl to make the puppet's face, then add the dress.

'I have taken this ordinary wooden spoon which makes the head and body of the puppet and fixed this plywood cross bar for the arms... if I work this wire rod up and down, the arms move. Eyes, nose and mouth for the puppet are made from gummed paper shapes... watch how the face is detailed as I stick the pieces to the underside of the spoon. Now I add the dress and you can see how the figure is taking form. A hat—made from bits of felt and knitting wool—is added to complete the puppet. Ladies and Gentlement... meet Tessa, the school terror!'

Place the puppet on the table and pick up the paper square, holding it fully open and with the eyes facing towards the audience.

'Tessa keeps a pet owl at school... she feeds it from her tuck box and has drawn eyes on this paper napkin... to see it through the week! Let me show you how to fold up a paper puppet... and dress it in a pocket handkerchief!'

Fold back the corners in the first operation then turn the packet over and continue the folds... if the paper has been well creased beforehand the folding becomes quite automatic. Insert the fingers as described and make the head by bending the folds forward.

'Last week, Tessa and her owl took part in the school concert... now let me show you how the puppets come to life with music and movement behind the screen... Tessa will recite for you and later the owl will sing!'

The sketch shows how the complete paper owl is formed with the handkerchief draped over the wrist and the two

A Rod Puppet Show

puppets are then taken back screen ready for the show. Place the handkerchief and paper head on a chair and raise Tessa into view on her own—holding the spoon handle in one hand and the wire operating rod with the other. Make the puppet bow and wiggle her arms as you say, using a high-pitched voice:

> 'I'm Tessa the fifth form terror,
> A terrible terror indeed!
> My teachers all tell me I'm not very bright
> And my hair hangs down like a weed!'

Here, the spoon handle is twisted back and forth quickly to make the woollen locks swing out. During the second verse, Tessa moves her arms and is made to walk from side to side of the screen in a series of bobs and hops finishing in a quick about-turn.

> 'I'm not very good at tennis,
> I'm not very fast on the track,
> Last week in the hurdle . . . I busted my girdle
> And met myself . . . on the way back!'

At the end of the second verse, the puppet is drawn down so that the owl puppet can be set up on the right hand ready for showing at the end of the third verse. The wooden spoon is grasped in the left hand and the index finger of this hand is placed into the wire loop for single-handed operation of the puppet. Tessa is quickly lifted into view again saying:

> 'But there's one little school friend I cherish,
> I'll keep him by fair means or foul,
> He's my little pet . . . you have not yet met,
> I'll fetch him . . . here's Ozzy the Owl!'

Bring the owl into action and let the two puppets perform a few lines of cross-talk patter and quips, synchronizing the jaw movements of the paper puppet with the dialogue.

A Rod Puppet Show

TESSA: Let me test your I.Q. Ozzy . . . answer the following questions. Where did the first tree grow?
OZZY: In the ground!
TESSA: What do you call a horse that collects coins?
OZZY: A hobby horse!
TESSA: What kind of pets are made of wood?
OZZY: Pup-pets!
TESSA: Oh Ozzy! I've taught you everything I know . . . and you still know nothing! You had better sing us a song!

The owl puppet sings the chorus of a popular song using wide, exaggerated jaw movements. The Al Jolson hit 'Mammy' is particularly suitable and gives great comic effect. The performer can either use his own singing voice or cut in a recording of the song. At the end, both puppets bow and disappear behind the screen.

THE PROFESSOR CONDUCTS

The head puppet is quickly tied in place round the performer's chin and, without any announcement, pops up above the screen. He raps his baton on the top of the screen and speaks:

'I am the school's music professor . . . and we will conclude the concert with a lively brass band march! Attention everybody! One . . . two . . . three . . . four!'

A recording of a Sousa-type march is started and the puppet conducts in vigorous fashion for about a minute to bring the act to a brisk finish. The performer comes round the screen—without the puppets—to take his bow.

The Skeleton in the Cupboard

Basic string puppetry is explained and taught with this easily built, 20-inch (500-mm.) skeleton marionette which performs in a home setting or on the stage of a portable, fold-up puppet theatre. Controls are simplified to give head, arm and leg movements but there is a moving jaw so that the marionette can be made to 'talk'. A complete routine involving the buried treasure of pirate Captain Kidd, with supplementary characters, is included and the act builds up to an amusing finish with the appearance of the captain and his parrot inside the treasure box.

A Portable String Puppet Theatre

The three main frames are built from lengths of 2-inch (50-mm.) by 1-inch (25-mm.) section planed timber using screwed half joints as the method of assembly. Each frame is 3 feet (900 mm.) high with the back panel measuring 4 feet (1,200 mm.) across and the side wings 2 feet (600 mm.) wide. Glue and screw the corners strongly then hinge the frames using two pairs of brass butts 3 inches (75 mm.) by ¾ inch (18 mm.) size. Two bars to carry the front opening curtains and the fixed upper drape are supported on two 3-foot (900 mm.)-long rising extensions which are bolted to the wing frames as shown. Coachbolts with wingnuts are used to attach the extensions which are given a 6-inch (150-mm.) overlap. The crossbar to carry the opening curtains is 4 feet 2 inches (1,250 mm.) long while the

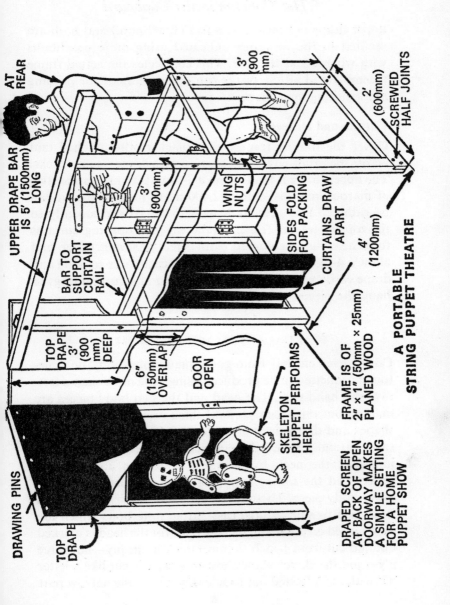

upper drape bar measures 5 feet (1,500 mm.) and both are secured in the positions indicated using more coachbolts with wingnuts at the rear. This completes the actual frame assembly and all the pieces can be taken apart for priming and painting matt black.

Curtain and Drapes

Cover the folding frames with black cloth stretched taut across the inside edges and secured with dome-headed tacks. The upper drape is made from a 3-foot (900 mm.)-wide strip of maroon material 8 feet (2,400 mm.) long so that it can be gathered into neat folds as it is tacked permanently to the top bar of the frame. Make the two opening curtains from heavy gold-coloured cloth 3 feet (900 mm.) deep and allow a 4-foot (1,200 mm.)-width for each piece to hang and drape easily without pulling. Use a rod and curtain rings to hang the pieces.

MAKING A SKELETON MARIONETTE

Constructed entirely from good quality plywood, the skeleton marionette can be produced using little more than a fretsaw and hand drill. The head and the two body pieces are marked out on $\frac{3}{8}$-inch (9-mm.) thick multi plywood to the shapes and dimensions given on the drawing and are then sawn carefully round the outlines. Notice how the head is joined at the neck by means of a tongue and grooved socket and the same method of joining is used to fix the lower body piece. These joints are carefully drilled through from side to side to take easy fitting long bolts which are then nutted on the screwed end. A jaw for the head is marked out and cut from $\frac{1}{4}$-inch (6-mm.) thick multi ply—not three ply—and the sketch shows how this piece is cut like a letter 'U' with teeth fretted out to fit easily across the narrow part

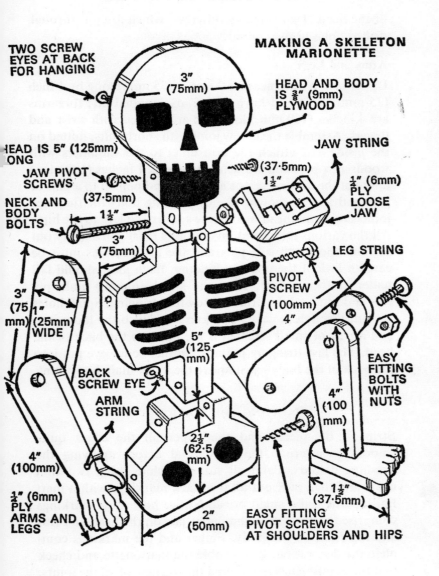

The Skeleton in the Cupboard

of the head. Two small woodscrews which are put through drilled holes in the jaw sides act as pivots.

Arms and Legs

Upper arm pieces measure 3 inches (75 mm.) long by 1 inch (25 mm.) wide and have both ends rounded off; forearms are 4 inches (100 mm.) long and are shaped with wrist and fingers. Assemble the elbow joint with short bolts, nutted on the inside and attach the arm units to the shoulders with woodscrew pivot pins. Each leg piece is 4 inches (100 mm.) long but the lower sections are glued and pinned to a pair of plywood feet as shown. Use easy fitting bolts for the knee joints and roundhead woodscrews to fix the legs to the hips. All the various joints and pivot points must work freely but without too much side play and the drilled holes must be eased a little if there is any binding. Each joint should fall under its own weight. Then the ¼-inch (6-mm.) multi ply legs and arms can be drilled ready for stringing. Small holes are put through in wrists and knees and also the loose jaw, and a pair of small screw eyes are put into the back of the head. The last stringing point is another screw eye put into the back of the body—just above the lower main body joint.

Painting the Marionette

Strip all the pieces and sandpaper all the edges quite smooth then prime the new wood before applying the finishing colours. Paint all surfaces white using two thin coats and then pick out all the black markings with a matt finish paint and a small brush. Notice how these markings comprise the eyes, nose and under-jaw on the head and ribs and hip joint on the body. Finger and toe markings complete the decoration. Reassemble the marionette and check that the painting has not altered the freeness of all the joints.

The Skeleton in the Cupboard

Control Bar

This is a vertical type of control bar giving a wide range of movements but the dimensions must be followed closely for the best results. The unit is built up on a 9-inch (225-mm.) length of inch-square (25 mm.) planed wood starting with the triangular base which is cut from ¼-inch (6-mm.) thick plywood. Mark off the three hole centres first—at 3-inch (75-mm.) spacings—then saw out the triangle on the outside of these stringing holes. Screw the ply piece to the base of the centre stick with one edge of the triangle facing forward as indicated. The arm bar is added next and this is made from a 12-inch (300-mm.) strip of ¼-inch (6-mm.) ply—tapered from the middle and with rounded-off ends. It is screwed to the top of the main stick and a pair of small screw eyes are inserted at the arm ends. The leg operating bar is of similar construction but is 10 inches (250 mm.) long and is mounted to the main stick in a different fashion. A wooden spacing block 1 inch (25 mm.) long is screwed to the control bar 6 inches (150 mm.) up from the base and a screw eye is twisted into the centre of this. Using a pair of pliers, the screw eye is carefully opened to make a right-angled hook and the leg bar is fixed on to this hook after drilling a central hole. The leg operating bar is worked either on the pin—to give a limited amount of movement to the legs—or off the pin to obtain the full walking action. Small holes are drilled in the ends of the leg bar for stringing the figure. Operation of the jaw is achieved with a string running through a screw eye and terminating in a thumb ring which is actuated by the hand holding the control bar. Finish the unit by inserting a hanging hook in the top end of the stick using a good-sized cup hook for the purpose. This hook is needed for stringing the marionette and also

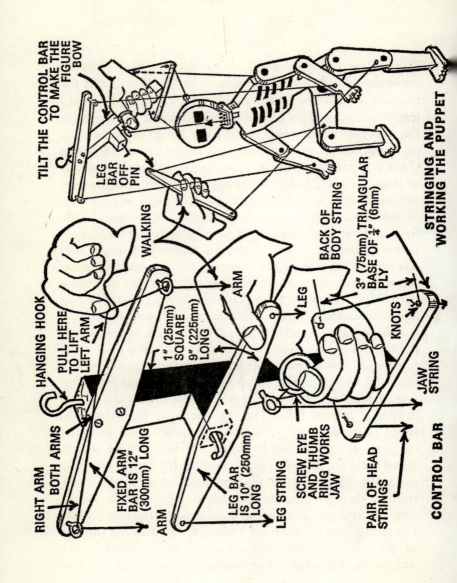

The Skeleton in the Cupboard

comes in useful for hanging the figure without tangling the cords prior to a performance. Sandpaper all the parts of the control bar and it can be left without painting.

STRINGING AND WORKING THE PUPPET

Eight strings connect the control bar to the marionette and these are added in a definite order. Since the control bar is manipulated at elbow height the lengths of the various strings will differ to suit each performer and the best method of setting is to hang the control bar at working height while the strings are being tied. Fix a hook to a suitable wooden post and hang the bar vertically then the first two strings can be added. These connect the two screw eyes at the back of the skeleton's head to the front pair of holes in the triangular base of the control bar and they should be tied off equally so that the figure is hanging with its feet just touching the floor. The next string is knotted into the back hole of the triangular base and is tied into the screw eye at the back of the body—still keeping the marionette hanging vertically. A single long string is used to operate the arms and this is first tied to one wrist, threaded up and through the two screw eyes in the fixed arm bar and then tied off at the other wrist, leaving the arms just slightly raised. The jaw string is first tied to the thumb ring and then threaded down through the screw eye in the front of the control bar before fixing to the moveable jaw and the length should be adjusted to give a comfortable operation before tying off. Finally, the leg strings are added with the leg bar on its central hook. Set the string lengths equally with the leg bar in a horizontal position and adjust so that the knees are just forward of centre. The sketches indicate the basic movements that can be given to the marionette and these should be practised until a degree of proficiency is attained. At first, thin black string should be used for the operating cords as these are not so inclined to tangle; later very fine nylon strings can be used to give an almost invisible operation.

Body Control

Grasp the control bar just above the base plate and insert the thumb through the jaw cord ring. Hold the marionette with its feet just touching the floor and notice that, with the control bar held vertically, all the string settings remain constant and the figure stays in a natural position. Tilt the bar forward and see how the figure follows suit in a bowing action then rock the bar from side to side to give an eccentric sideways movement to the puppet. You can make the figure sit down by lowering the control bar and keeping the weight on its feet causing the knees to bend. The real secret of string marionette control comes from moderate manipulation of the cords and watching the figure closely . . . letting the puppet stand on its own feet and doing what comes naturally. Operate the jaw in a steady series of opening and closing movements during the dialogue but no great attempt at exact synchronization is required.

Arm Movements

The drawing shows how either arm is raised by lifting the long string near to the appropriate screw eye. Both arms can be elevated together when the string is pulled from the centre of the arm bar.

Leg Actions and Walking

There are three methods of operating the legs—by pulling the strings individually for single action, by rocking the leg bar about the central pivot to make the figure mark time on the spot and the full walking action when the leg bar is lifted off the hook completely and is actuated by the other

The Skeleton in the Cupboard

hand as shown. The leg bar is held about 12 inches (300 mm.) in front of the main control unit and both hands move in unison while still retaining this distance. Rock the leg bar from side to side to make the puppet step out at walking pace.

THE TREASURE CHEST

Captain Kidd's treasure chest is made entirely from ¼-inch (6-mm.) thick plywood and measures 14 inches (350 mm.) long by 8 inches (200 mm.) wide and 8 inches (200 mm.) deep. Use panel pins and glue to assemble the pieces and hinge the lid as shown with a pair of small brass butts fitted behind the box and to the underside of the flap. Both the pirate and the parrot figures are sawn from ply pieces measuring 6 inches (150 mm.) by 4 inches (100 mm.) after marking the outlines as drawn. These two cut-outs are fixed into the box behind the front panel using easy fitting pivot bolts nutted on the inside. Notice how the figures are mounted with the pivot points off centre so that both pirate and parrot fall back into the box when the operating strings are released. Captain Kidd is painted with moustache, eye patch and hat bearing the skull and crossbones and the parrot is a bright yellow with red beak. Before painting prime all the new wood. Paint the treasure chest brown and add the ornamental metalwork—lock and corner plates—in gold. Write the name Capt. Kidd 1670 under the lock. Three cords operate the box and its figures—one is knotted through a hole in the corner of the lid and the others are tied to the cut-out heads.

SETTING UP THE SHOW

A simple setting for a home puppet show can be constructed using an open doorway covered part-way down with a cur-

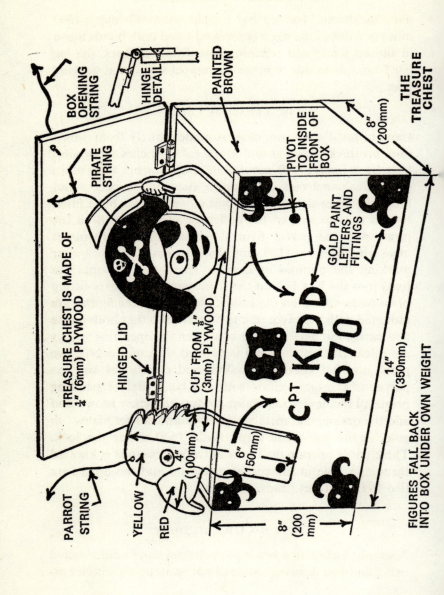

The Skeleton in the Cupboard

tain affixed by drawing-pins; the gap between the bottom of this drape and the floor should be 2 feet 9 inches (825 mm.). The backing screen can be a clothes drying frame of the folding variety covered with black cloth and the string marionette is worked in front of this screen. The operator is, of course, masked from view by the door top drape. The show can be set up with the door closed then, when everyone is ready, the door is opened to reveal the skeleton in the cupboard. To perform the full pirate routine, the treasure chest is placed centre stage against the backcloth and the skeleton is folded inside with the string carefully draped and the lid closed. The operating strings for the box lid and parrot and pirate are hung over the back rail of the puppet theatre.

Performing the Show: What to Say and Do

The main curtains are opened to reveal the treasure chest and the performer sets the scene with a few lines of introductory patter:

'Three centuries ago, the pirate buccaneer Captain William Kidd buried looted treasure on an unknown island in the Caribbean Sea and the secret location of this hidden wealth has remained a mystery since the death of the Captain soon afterwards. The brass-bound treasure chest still lies unclaimed and unopened on a sandy beach . . . just waiting for someone to discover its secret. But listen! . . . something is knocking inside the box!'

The performer raps his knucles a few times on the back frame then slowly pulls the box lid open. The skeleton is lifted into view, revealing first the head and then standing up in the chest. With a brisk jump, the figure leaps out of the box on to the stage and then the mouth is made to work as the performer speaks the dialogue in a high-pitched voice.

The Skeleton in the Cupboard

'Shiver me timbers!... I thought I was locked in that box for ever! As true as my name is Billy Bones I was sure that villain Captain Kidd would never set me free! Wait while I stretch my poor old bones... I can feel them creaking in every joint!'

Raise first one arm and then the other and then lift both up together. Operate the leg bar on its pivot and make Billy Bones lift his knees alternately—slowly at first and then quickening till he is marking time at a brisk pace. He halts, then points at the box.

'I was ship's cook aboard the pirate galleon when we sailed under the king's orders to spoil and plunder on the Spanish Main... but Kidd turned traitor to his country and made dishonest men of us all! His loot is in that box... and he left me here to guard it! I remember how Kidd marked it on his map... six paces north and five paces east!'

The leg bar is removed from the hook and the puppet is made to walk six long steps across the stage and then five more paces to the side of the box. The marionette jumps up and sits on the edge of the treasure chest.

'We buried the box at this spot but a typhoon must have blown the sand away. It seems like only yesterday when me and my shipmates rowed to the island to hide the treasure for Kidd. We were a merry crew after drinking our tots of rum and often danced the Sailor's Hornpipe... like this!'

A realistic hornpipe dance can be imparted to the puppet by raising the arms one after the other and making the figure hop, first on one leg and then the other, in time to a musical jig which can be whistled by the performer or provided by piano or record. At the end of this dance, the puppet flops down on the stage and sits with outstretched legs.

'Golly, I feel tired!... as though I hadn't had anything to eat for three hundred years! I wonder what happened to

The Skeleton in the Cupboard

that scoundrel Captain Kidd? I'm sure his ghost must haunt this island!'

At this point in the routine, the pirate cut-out is suddenly lifted into view and the performer speaks in a different voice to simulate the Captain's deep-toned commands:

'Bones! Bones! . . . I'll call you Idle Bones! Why aren't you guarding my treasure!'

Immediately, the pirate cut-out is allowed to fall back into the box and the parrot makes a quick appearance, to repeat the line of patter but in a squeaky tone. This interplay continues with, first, the Captain bobbing up to shout something and then the Parrot appearing for a few seconds to repeat—parrot fashion—the Captain's lines, as follows:

'Bones! . . . is that you answering back! I'll break every bone in your body!' (Parrot repeats.)

'I'll make you walk the plank! . . . you prattling pirate! I'll run you through with my cutlass!' (Parrot repeats.)

'It must be an echo! . . . one . . . two . . . three!'

The Parrot is lifted into view and both cut-outs stay in sight as the final line of this 'echo' patter is delivered by the Parrot.

'It must be an echo! . . . four . . . five . . . six!'

The string marionette is raised to its feet and the jaw is operated by the thumb ring while the left hand holds both strings of the box cut-out figures. Manipulating more than one figure with only two hands is straightforward if the action is concentrated on one puppet at a time with the other marionette resting. Mr. Bones speaks:

'So! . . . the tables are turned Captain Kidd! Like me . . . you and your talking parrot are doomed to stay castaways on this island for ever! Get back in that box and I'll join you to slumber for another three hundred years! But first a song! . . .

The Skeleton in the Cupboard

'Fifteen men on a dead man's chest,
Yo ho! . . . and a bottle of rum!
Drink and the devil has done the rest!
Yo Ho! . . . and a bottle of rum!'

After the two cut-outs have been lowered back into the chest, the left hand is free to remove the leg bar and walk the skeleton across the stage towards the box. Billy Bones turns to face the audience and raises his arm in salute—the leg bar is re-hung on its pin permitting the left hand to operate one arm. The puppet crouches, then leaps into the chest and stands to sing the song. Finally, he is lowered out of sight and the lid is closed. Draw the front curtains and walk round from behind to thank your audience.

An Evening With Puppets

Most of the routines can be assembled to provide a complete puppet variety show and there are several combinations that the entertainer can choose to suit the type of audience and the location of the show. For a home presentation, where the audience is very near the performer, the first programme is ideal. The performer can present the routines exactly as written using only his spoken voice.

A Home Presentation

1. A Finger Puppet Theatre
2. TV Shadow Puppets
3. A Punch and Judy Show

The amateur entertainer is often engaged to appear at larger functions such as church socials and school concerts and it is here that an introductory act like the Rod Puppet Show is particularly valuable since it presents the performer face to face with his audience and allows him to establish his identity as the puppet master. As well as the tape recordings needed for this first routine, the patter and sound effects for the TV Shadow Puppets can also be pre-recorded so that the performer only has to create the shadows in time with the tape. Sounds such as steam locomotives, car engines, cheering crowds and music to suit the mood of the particular scene all add to the effectiveness of the routine; it is the technique of the cartoon film maker, and can serve as a useful introduction to this fascinating side of the craft. The string marionette routine brings this show to a close and music to accompany the skeleton during the hornpipe dance can finish off the tape. Lighting in the typical village hall can be a problem because puppets need plenty of frontal illuminations. Separate footlights can be carried on a portable batten but the best method is a fixed spotlight mounted out in the hall.

CHURCH HALL CONCERT

1. A Rod Puppet Show
2. TV Shadow Puppets
3. The Skeleton in the Cupboard (Captain Kidd's Treasure)

Three individual routines are used for this big stage show and there is a short interval before the last item to give the performer time to apply the clown make-up for the surprising living marionette finish. The stage is first set with folding screen and table for the rod puppets on one side and the Punch booth on the other. During the interval, the stage curtains are drawn and the living marionette theatre is set ready with the performer standing behind. When this act is finished, the performer can remove the body of the living marionette from his neck and walk round to face the audience, still wearing the face of the clown.

BIG STAGE SHOW

1. A Rod Puppet Show
2. A Punch and Judy Show
   Interval
3. Living Marionettes (Clown in a Circus)

- 6. NOV. 1972

- 9. JAN. 1976

15. APR. 1977

- 2. NOV. 1979

14 DEC. 1979

19. FEB. 1980

- 1. JUL. 1980

23 FEB 1983

SURREY COUNTY LIBRARY
(Headquarters, 140 High Street, Esher)

72-189509

This book must be returned to the Branch or Travelling Library from which is was borrowed, by the latest date entered above.

Charges will be payable on books kept overdue.